Reykjavík
The Blue Lagoon
Snæfellsjökull
Ísafjörður
Hvítserkur
Drangey
Akureyri
Dettifoss
Mývatn
Seyðisfjörður

Jökulsárlón
Skaftafell
Dyrhólaey
Landmannalaugar
Skógafoss
Thórsmörk
Eyjafjallajökull
Vestmannaeyjar
Geysir
Gullfoss

Reykjavík

In the capital of Iceland you can find an interesting mix of the small nation living on this volcanic island. Reykjavík is a vibrant city that offers everything you can dream of when it comes to entertainment, culture and art. The city's tallest building is Hallgrímskirkja, which is also the tallest church in the country. There is a fantastic view of Reykjavik from the tower, of the blue waters and beautiful mountains surrounding the city. The people of Iceland are lucky to have ample hot water and geothermal energy, and in Reykjavik alone, there are seven outdoor geothermal swimming pools with facilities for children, where you can swim in the warm water, enjoy a sauna or simply sit and relax in the hot pots. Donald and his nephews feel right at home in Reykjavík. Actually, they like it so much that they are thinking of following in the footsteps of Ingólfur Arnarson and settle there for good!

Interesting facts:

- Ingólfur Arnarson is considered to be the first permanent settler in Iceland. He settled in Reykjavík in 870.
- Steam from nearby hot springs inspired the name of Reykjavík, which literally means "Smoke Bay".
- Population: Reykjavík has around 118.000 inhabitants and 2/3 of the country's population live in the greater capital area.
- Reykjavík is home to the oldest consecutive parliament in the world.
- Because of the Gulf Stream, the climate of Reykjavík is considerably warmer than in most other places on the same latitude of the planet.

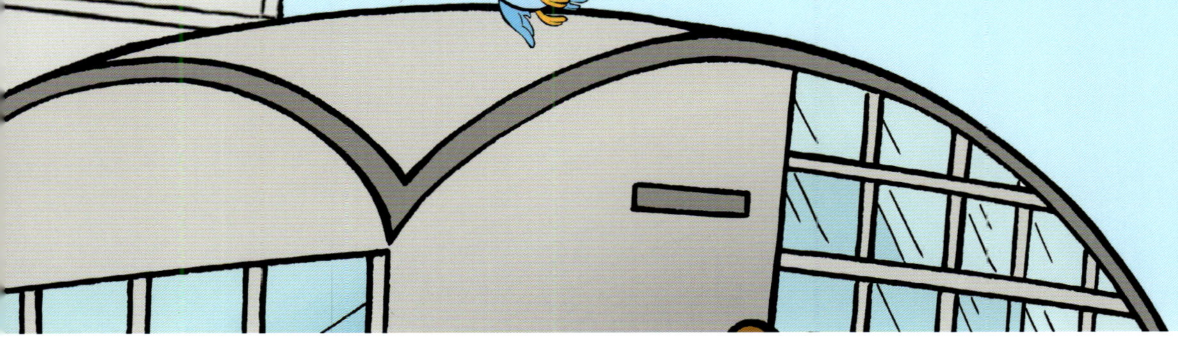

The Blue Lagoon

This is the best place to splash in the water and dabble in the mud for fun and good health! The Blue Lagoon is a fantastic world famous spa. The Lagoon's geothermal seawater contains a special mix of minerals, silica and algae that are famous for their positive effects on the skin and the blue water is renowned for its healing power. This makes bathing in the Blue Lagoon an absolutely magical experience, and no wonder it is one of the most popular places for tourists to visit in Iceland. Huey, Dewey and Louie seem to be having a great time! Or maybe it is the Lagoon's rejuvenating power... perhaps the picture is really of Donald Duck and Scrooge McDuck?

Interesting facts:

- The geothermal seawater in the Lagoon comes directly from 2000 m deep boreholes.
- The water is rich in minerals, silica and algae.
- The temperature of the water is 37-39°C or 99-102°F
- The Lagoon contains 6 million litres of subterranean seawater that renews itself entirely every 40 hours.
- The Blue Lagoon is situated in between two continents, as the Eurasian and American tectonic plates meet at the Lagoon.

Snæfellsjökull

Donald feels right at home here! Snæfellsjökull glacier is magical and renowned for its special power. The glacier has always been a mystical place and many people claim it is home to supernatural beings such as the famous hidden people of Iceland. Some even think that the glacier is a popular destination for extraterrestrial beings and in the 1990s a group of people actually organised a reception for aliens that were said to have announced their visit! Unfortunately, they didn't show up for their own party, – at least not this time. Notwithstanding these legends, it is the breathtaking beauty of the glacier rather than its mystical power that attracts people and Snæfellsjökull is a very popular destination for visitors. Donald and Daisy really know how to make the most of what the glacier has to offer! Even though Donald's attitude sometimes gets on Daisy's nerves, their trip to the glacier will be unforgettable.

Interesting facts:

- Snæfellsjökull is an ancient stratovolcano on the westernmost tip of the Snæfellsnes peninsula, created by volcanic and phreatic eruptions during the last 700 thousand years.
- Height: 1.446 metres.
- Distance from Reykjavík: about 180 km.
- Scene of Jules Verne's book *A Journey to the Centre of the Earth.*
- The only national park in Iceland that stretches from the mountains to the sea.

Ísafjörður

Donald has definitely come here to sing! There is something very special about the landscape and vegetation of the West fjords. The fjords are narrow and deep, with high, steep mountains all around, and the distance between the mountains and the sea is incredibly short. Numerous historical sites and natural wonders like the amazing Dynjandi waterfall give a distinct character to the area. Most of the inhabitants of the Ísafjörður region live in or around Ísafjörður, which is actually the principal town of the region. There is no shortage of cultural life here and there is always something happening on the music scene. As a matter of fact, the first music school in the country was founded here in 1911. The annual music festival *I Never Went South* attracts a number of famous musicians and a huge crowd of music enthusiasts – you don't want to miss it!

Interesting facts:

- Flight time from Reykjavík is 40 minutes.
- It is possible to sail from Ísafjörður through the bay of Djúp into the Hornstrandir reserve.
- The main skiing resorts of the Ísafjörður area, and among the best ones in Iceland, are in the valleys of Tungudalur and Seljalandsdalur.
- The fishing industry has always been extremely important for the people of Ísafjörður.
- Kaldbakur is the highest mountain in the West fjords, 998 metres high.

Hvítserkur

Run, Donald, the troll is chasing you! Hvítserkur is an incredibly beautiful cliff, moulded by sea erosion and rising 15 metres out of the sea, deep in the western part of Húnafjörður. Bird droppings cover the cliff and give it its characteristic white hue which probably inspired its name. The sea erosion has carved holes through its foundations and sculptured it in the shape of a petrified monster. According to an old legend, Hvítserkur used to be a huge troll that set out to smash a loud bell that was chiming in the neighbourhood, when the sun came up and turned it into stone, which is often the fate of Icelandic trolls that are hit by the rays of the morning sun. It is very interesting to go down to the shore to get a closer look at the cliff or simply to explore the beach.

Interesting facts:

- Hvítserkur is located on the eastern part of Vatnsnes, about 50 km from the town of Blönduós.
- Road number 711 leads to Hvítserkur.
- A few bird species nest on the steep cliff and the cormorant is the most common bird there.

Drangey

Drangey island is a majestic rock formation of volcanic tuff in the middle of Skagafjörður. Huey, Dewey and Louie want to know everything about the interesting history of Drangey, which goes way back. The highest point of the island reaches 180 metres above sea level and there is only one access point. Do you want to know how this awesome rock fortress was formed? An old folktale tells the story of two giant night-prowling trolls, a man and a woman, that were crossing the fjord with their cow at daybreak. As the sun came up, all three of them were turned into stone. According to the legend, Drangey represents the cow and Kerling (the female troll) is to the south of it, but Karlinn (the male troll) that used to stand on its north side has disappeared into the sea. Drangey was first mentioned in Grettis saga as the refuge of the strong outlaw Grettir, who spent his last years there with his brother and their slave, and was killed on the island. Climbing Drangey is not recommended if you are afraid of heights, but it is a breathtaking experience. It is truly unforgettable, to stand on the top at sunset on a bright summer night, contemplating the fantastic view over the fjord with its villages and farms.

Interesting facts:

- Drangey used to be an important food supply for the people of Skagafjörður fjord for ages, providing fowl and eggs. The bird life on the island is very lively and there is still some bird hunting.
- Boats sail out to the island from Reykjar and Hofsós.
- There is a ladder for climbing the most difficult parts and the path is marked with rope and metal rails.

Akureyri

This thriving town, sometimes called the capital of the North, is a popular destination for visitors as it offers numerous possibilities for sightseeing and fun and is very close to many of Iceland's most stunning places. In summer, a visit to the beautiful park in the centre or playing golf in the midnight sun can be recommended. Akureyri is equally interesting in winter, especially for ski enthusiasts like Donald, as the town boasts one of the most popular skiing resorts in Iceland. After a fun-filled day of skiing in Hlíðarfjall mountain or exploring some historical place, there is nothing like relaxing in the hot pots of the local swimming pool. Do not miss climbing the stairs to the Akureyri church – and counting them on the way up. Actually, the figures provided by those that have climbed the stairs and counted them vary from 95 to 116!

Interesting facts:

- The bus ride on the local bus in Akureyri is free!
- Akureyri is the largest town outside of the capital area.
- Population: 18 000.
- The islands Grímsey and Hrísey belong to the municipality of Akureyri.
- The polar circle cuts through the northern part of Grímsey.

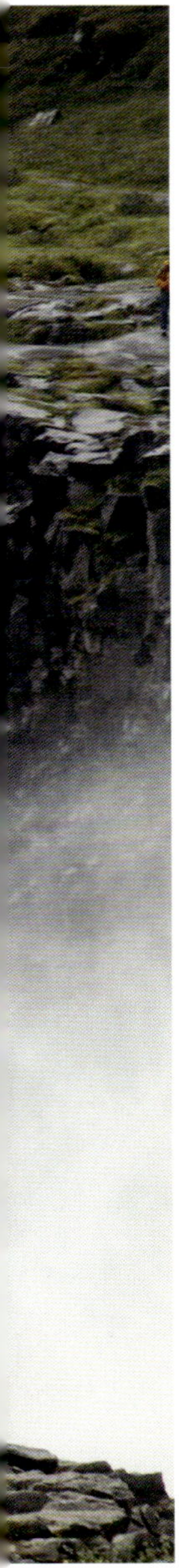

Dettifoss

Better be careful here! This magnificent waterfall in the Jökulsárgljúfur canyon is 44 metres high and reputedly the most powerful waterfall in Europe. To witness its amazing power is an unforgettable experience which has inspired many poets as well as musical composers. Water, sand and mud rush down the canyon with a thundering force, generating a drizzle displaying all the colours of the rainbow on a fine day; an experience that leaves no one untouched. However tempting it may seem to go right to the edge to look down, Huey, Dewey and Louie better be careful when walking on the edge of the canyon, as it is quite slippery.

Interesting facts:

- Dettifoss is in the Vatnajökull national park, 90 km from Húsavík.
- Dettifoss is the centre fall in a unique series of waterfalls; about 1 km to the south is Selfoss, and Hafragilsfoss is in the canyon about 2 km down the river.
- A marked trail leads up to Selfoss and the hike back and forth takes about one hour.
- Down on the flat riverbank there are marked paths and a viewing platform.

Mývatn

The midges rule lake Mývatn in summer and you better be ready to take them on! However, the midges that give the lake its name shouldn't prevent anyone from enjoying this remarkable place and its exceptional beauty. Craters and volcanoes have sculpted the landscape of the Mývatn region, many of which are famous spots, e.g. the volcanic craters of Krafla and Hverfjall. There is a long tradition of bathing in geothermal water in the region and the latest addition is the Mývatn Nature Baths. The Mývatn region is a world of adventure and natural wonders. Don't miss one of its most spectacular places, Dimmuborgir, made up of volcanic rock formations created about 2300 years ago.

Interesting facts:

- Mývatn is the fourth largest lake in Iceland, 37 square kilometres, dotted with more than 40 islands and islets.
- Mývatn is probably best known for its varied birdlife and more species of duck are said to live there than in any other place on earth.

Seyðisfjörður

Seyðisfjörður is an important tourist destination as well as a harbour for Norræna, the only car and passenger ferry that sails weekly between Iceland and the continent of Europe. The ferry is slightly more modern than Donald's vessel, as Donald prefers style to modern comfort. The town, which is surrounded by tall, majestic mountains, has a long and remarkable story as can be seen from its picturesque old wooden buildings. The town has many intriguing sights, among them the beautiful Blue Church located in the heart of town. The church has a remarkable story and for some reason, it is positioned in a reverse manner compared to other churches in Iceland.

Interesting facts:

- The population of Seyðisfjörður is around 700.
- Fishing and fish processing have always been the most important industry but tourism is constantly growing in importance.
- Some of the works of the world-renowned artist Dieter Roth are on display in the Skaftafell cultural centre. Dieter, who died in 1998, lived and worked in Seyðisfjörður during the last years of his life.

Jökulsárlón

This old boot is probably the only thing left for Donald to catch with his old hook in Jökulsárlón glacier lagoon. There is hardly a more magnificent place to go fishing even though there is no guarantee that you will catch anything! The glacier lagoon is truly a spectacular natural wonder with an air of adventure about it, with its black sand and rocks set against majestic icebergs of various shapes and forms floating around the turquoise lagoon. Shoals of herring and capelin are carried into Jökulsárlón by the waves and the seals follow the food and can be seen loitering around the lagoon. Maybe Donald gets lucky with his fishing if he waits long enough!

Interesting facts:

- Jökulsárlón is the deepest lake in Iceland, 248 m deep.
- Jökulsárlón is located on Breiðamerkursandur just off route number 1, about 60 km east of Skaftafell and 80 km to the west of the town of Höfn.
- Visitors can go on a boat trip on the lagoon every day in summer.

Skaftafell

Who says there are no trees in Iceland? Skaftafell national park in the Vatnajökull reserve contains some of Iceland's most precious natural treasures. Its unique natural beauty, favourable weather conditions and a variety of hiking trails make Skaftafell one of the most popular destinations for visitors that want to enjoy the outdoors in an area that has no roads apart from paths leading up to local farms. There is no need for Donald to be so surprised with this single tree he found, who knows, he might run into some more on his stroll around the area?

Interesting facts:

- Skaftafell belongs to the Vatnajökull reserve, the largest national park in Europe.
- Distance from Reykjavík: 327 km.
- 2/3 of Vatnajökull glacier are within the national park.
- The total size of the national park is 4807 square kilometres.
- Skaftafell is home to over 250 different plants and about 30 bird species nest there.

Dyrhólaey

Donald is in trouble now! Dyrhólaey is a 120 metre high promontory on the south coast of Iceland, forming the southernmost part of the mainland. Even though the ending of its name in Icelandic (-ey) might indicate it is an island, it is really a promontory that reaches out into the ocean. Because of the arch-shaped opening the cape is often called Portland in old foreign maps. Boats can sail through the arch and a small plane was once flown through it. No one has ever flown through on an air mattress and even though it looks like Donald is about to try that, it is not recommended. The ocean currents are extremely strong and dangerous in this area so Huey, Dewey and Louie better be very careful on the black sand!

Interesting facts:

- Dyrhólaey was formed in an underwater volcanic eruption about 80 thousand years ago.
- A lighthouse was originally built on the cape in 1910 whereas the current lighthouse was erected in 1927.
- There are cliffs and pillars to the south of Dyrhólaey, the highest one is Háidrangur at 56 m.
- This is a paradise for bird watchers as various species of seabirds live on the cape itself and its surrounding rock pillars.
- Dyrhólaey is protected during nesting season.

Landmannalaugar

It's good to know that the Junior Woodchucks have had first-aid training! They are in Landmannalaugar, a highland paradise in a valley surrounded by mountains. Hot and cold springs emerge from under the lava, creating a warm pool called Laugalækur, which is equally awesome for bathing on bright summer nights as on dark winter nights when the northern lights dance around the starry sky. All this natural beauty is making Donald gasp, but he will hopefully get over it soon.

Interesting facts:

- A very active geothermal area, which is connected to one of the country's largest high temperature geothermal area, the Torfajökull glacier area.
- The Landmannalaugar area, at 600 m above sea level, has multicoloured mountains and equally colourful rocks, including volcanic glass, rhyolit and rhyolit lava.
- A very popular hiking trail called Laugavegur runs between Landmannalaugar and Thórsmörk.
- There are huts offering accommodation that need to be booked well in advance. There is also a rather rocky camping area, so it can be difficult to drive the pegs into the ground.

Skógafoss

Did Scrooge McDuck hit jackpot? The tall and majestic Skógafoss waterfall, one of the most beautiful waterfalls in Iceland, falls off the edge of the cliffs at Skógar on the south coast of Iceland. A legend has it that the first Viking settler in the area, Thrasi Thórólfsson, buried a chest of gold in a cave behind the waterfall, which can be seen glowing in the sun when the rainbow dances in the waterfall. Scrooge has obviously been blinded by the gold!

Interesting facts:

- Skógafoss has been declared a natural wonder and preserved from 1987.
- The waterfall is 60 m high and 25 m wide.
- Skógafoss falls from Skógá River, which originates from two places; from under Eyjafjallajökull below Fimmvörðuháls and also from the western part of Mýrdalsjökull.
- There is a hiking trail to the east of the waterfall, leading over Fimmvörðuháls down into Thórsmörk.

Thórsmörk

The road to Thórsmörk is not for any ordinary cars and it is rather unlikely that Donald and his nephews will ever get there in this old ride! Thórsmörk is a popular destination for Icelandic visitors, who come to enjoy the fantastic wilderness, surrounded by mountains which ensure great weather conditions. There are numerous hiking trails in the area and you better look out for bouncing elves or fairies among the buttercups, moss and geraniums. The trails take you over deep rivers with strong currents, so you shouldn't venture there without an experienced guide.

Interesting facts:

- Distance from Reykjavík: 150 km.
- The name of Thórsmörk is inspired by Thor, the Nordic God.
- A popular hiking trail from Thórsmörk leads over the Fimmvörðuháls ridge, right where a volcanic eruption started on 20 March 2010.

Eyjafjallajökull

Everyone knows how unlucky Donald can be, but can you believe that he took his girlfriend on a picnic just as a volcano started erupting nearby!

Eyjafjallajökull was probably the hottest place in Iceland in spring 2010 and the effect of the Eyjafjallajökull eruption was truly widespread. Even though it annoyed many people that had to change their flight schedules around Europe, there were probably more people, all over the world, having fun trying to pronounce the name of Eyjafjallajökull – with interesting results, to say the least!

Interesting facts:

- One of the highest peaks of Iceland at 1.666 m.
- The country's fifth largest glacier.
- A stratovolcano located under the glacier has erupted four times since the settlement.
- Eyjafjallajökull is steep and has numerous fissures which makes it very dangerous for travellers who shouldn't venture there without an experienced guide.

Vestmannaeyjar

Perhaps the ducks got tired of volcanic eruptions and decided to head for Vestmannaeyjar? Maybe they aren't aware of the huge volcanic eruption that started in Heimaey in 1973 causing the entire population to be temporarily evacuated and transferred to the mainland. If you intend to visit, you better choose your outfit better than the ducks did if you don't want to startle the locals. The islands were attacked by pirates in the early 17th century, who abducted almost half of the inhabitants and took them to Algeria to sell them on a slave market. Despite their various misfortunes, the people of Vestmannaeyjar really know how to have a good time. Ask anyone to teach you how to swing on a rope from the cliffs, an experience you do not want to miss. If you prefer a less hazardous sport, you can always count puffins, as these little friendly seabirds live here by the millions. Are you ready to count?

Interesting facts:

- An archipelago south of Iceland, 15 islands in total.
- The islands were formed in a series of volcanic eruptions, the first ones about 12.000 years ago.
- Heimaey is the largest island and the only one that is populated.
- Population: about 4.100.

Geysir

No wonder Scrooge McDuck brought an umbrella, the water squirts all over the place! Even though the great hot spring Geysir has been rather quiet lately, it is truly worth to visit it and the large family of hot springs around it. There are numerous hot springs in the Geysir area and the second largest one, Strokkur, has taken over from Geysir as the most active one, erupting every 4-8 minutes up to 30 metres in the air. The great Geysir, undoubtedly the world's most famous hot spring, used to be very powerful and erupted at regular intervals, spouting boiling hot water up to 60-80 metres in the air.

Interesting facts:

- Geysir was sold in 1894 to an Irish monk for 3000 Icelandic crowns but ended up as public property in 1935.
- The English word for a hot spring is "geyser", derived from the name of the great Geysir.
- The Geysir area includes at least 30 hot springs and multicoloured streams.
- Geysir, together with Thingvellir national park and Gullfoss waterfall, make up the incredibly popular Golden Circle, the most frequented route for visitors in Iceland.

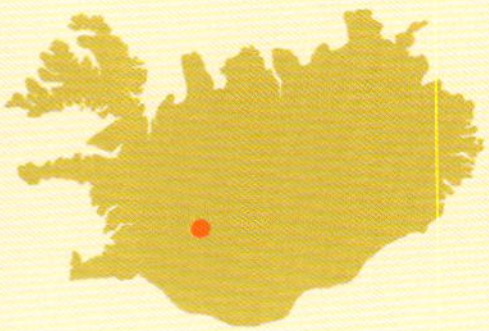

Gullfoss

Even though the name of Gullfoss waterfall could indicate that it is made of gold, Scrooge is disappointed to find out that it actually isn't. However, his disappointment quickly turns into delight when he visits Gullfoss, the king of Icelandic waterfalls, renowned for its spectacular beauty and an essential element of every visitor's itinerary in Iceland. Gullfoss has always been admired for its exceptional beauty and during the early 20th century it was also considered to be a feasible option for producing hydraulic power, which is the main source of electricity in Iceland. The preservation of Gullfoss waterfall was declared in 1978 and ever since, it has been popular with visitors that come to enjoy its magnificence, which is more precious than any worldly profit. This breathtaking waterfall is surely one of the most beautiful treasures of Icelandic nature.

Interesting facts:

- Gullfoss falls on two levels down 70 m into Hvítárgljúfur canyon.
- The upper part of the waterfall is 11 m high and the lower part about 21 m.
- Gullfoss is among the 10 most beautiful waterfalls in the world according to the CNN travel web in March 2011.
- Gullfoss plays the main role in the musical video *Heaven* by the band *Live*.

Have fun in Iceland!